WEIRD WONDERS AND BIZARRE BLUNDERS

The Official Book of Ridiculous Records

Brad Schreiber

Meadowbrook Press

Distributed by Simon & Schuster
New York

Library of Congress Cataloging-in-Publication Data

Schreiber, Brad

  Weird wonders and bizarre blunders: the official book of ridiculous records/
Brad Schreiber.
    p.   cm.
  Summary: A collection of fictitious world records, supposedly rejected by other record
books for being dangerous, moronic, or goofy, grouped in such areas as the human body
and artistic achievements.
  1. World records—Juvenile humor. 2. Curiosities and wonders—Juvenile humor.
3. Records—Miscellanea—Juvenile humor.
  [1. World records—Wit and humor.] I. Title.
  PN6231.W646S35   1989   813'.54—dc20   89-33911
  ISBN: 0-88166-174-0

Editor: Bruce Lansky
Production Editor: Sandy McCullough
Art Directors: Maria Mazzara, Sallie Baker
Production Manager: Pam Scheunemann

Simon & Schuster Ordering #: 0-671-69035-3

The following records copyright © 1989 by Bruce Lansky:Best-Mannered Parrot, Dog's
Best Friend, Dumbest April Fool's Joke, Dumbest Cow, Dumbest Opera, Fastest Car Jack,
Friendliest Giraffe, Happiest Artist, Largest Painting, Most Conniving Canines, Most Dan-
gerous Magician, Most Hazardous Lie, Most Annoying One-Man Band, Most Loving Son,
Most Spam Eaten, Oldest Memo, Shortest Tailor, Toughest Driving Test, Weirdest Lunch,
World's Fastest Typist, Documenting Your Records, Rules and Regulations, Communica-
tions About Your Record, and Publisher's Note.

All other records copyright © 1989 by Brad Schreiber.

Photo on p. 63 copyright © 1989 by Meadowbrook Photos.
Photo on p. 19 copyright © 1989 by Kenneth C. Poertner.
Photos on p. 72 copyright © 1989 by Maureen Murphy
Photos on pp. 7, 8, 9, 11, 43, 47, 56, copyright © 1989 Globe Photos, Inc.
Photos on pp. 10, 16, 18, 25, 32, 36, 46, 50, 64, 69, 73, 75, 81, 85, 87 copyright © 1989 by
Wide World Photos, Inc.

Published by Meadowbrook Press, 18318 Minnetonka Boulevard, Deephaven, MN 55391.

BOOK TRADE DISTRIBUTION by Simon & Schuster, a division of Simon and Schuster,
Inc., 1230 Avenue of the Americas, New York, NY 10020.

89 90 91 92 5 4 3 2 1

Printed in the United States of America.

To Andrew and the memory of Mona:
my teachers, my friends, my parents.

CONTENTS

How to Get Your Record Published in This Book

A Word About Record Books

This is not the only record book in existence. There are several others, some of which have enjoyed a certain degree of popularity over the years. The other record books automatically reject records that are moronic, pointless, and goofy. But what they reject, we publish, because our world is a strange and puzzling place—so why not publish strange and puzzling records? *Weird Wonders and Bizarre Blunders* is a lot more entertaining to read than the other record books...and, thanks to us, it's now a lot easier to set your own world record.

To get into the other record books, you have to break existing records. To get into ours, you can do that too, or you can attempt to do something no one in his or her right mind would do. If it's weird enough, you just might earn yourself a place in history.

Who's to Say What Is "Accepted"?

We say. It's our book. If you don't like it, see if the other record books will publish your accomplishments in juggling hamsters or staging the longest food fight in an expensive French restaurant. (Actually, both of these things would interest us.) So, go out, do something silly or strange and prove it to us. But don't do anything dangerous. We want you to live long enough to enjoy seeing your name in print.

Rules and Regulations

Everybody hates rules and regulations, right? So, let's keep them to a minimum. If your record involves a recognized world or national governing body for a particular activity, don't even bother. We're interested in activities that seem almost too ridiculous to be true.

If your record attempt can be classified as a "marathon," don't take any rest intervals during the attempt. The whole point of a marathon is to push the limits of human endurance, so don't complain and moan about being tired or having to go to the bathroom. Exhaustion and dirty underwear make the record attempt more worthy of publication.

We wish to emphasize that we cannot be held liable for any person who, during a record attempt for our book, causes bodily injury, private or public property damage, death, disfigurement, confusion, embarrassment, or mental breakdown. If setting your record isn't fun, don't do it. We don't want you to injure yourself or anyone else. There is enough misery in the world.

Documenting Your Record

1. Have your record witnessed by independent, impartial professionals who are well respected in your community, such as police officers, teachers, religious leaders, doctors, lawyers, psychologists, or experts in your field. We do not accept statements from witnesses currently serving time in jail or a mental institution, or from politicians.

2. Obtain independent corroboration of your record by local or national members of the press, including newspaper, magazine, radio or television reporters, and photographers. Please do not send clippings from tabloid newspapers specializing in stories about Elvis and UFO sightings, or diets that let you eat all the cake and ice cream you want.

3. Submit your record in writing, along with the signatures of all witnesses, photographs, and any press clippings.

4. Send a $10 entry fee. Make out your check to Meadowbrook Press, and send it in care of the Weird Wonders editor.

All submissions will become the property of the publisher. The publisher will attempt to return only those materials accompanied by a self-addressed, stamped envelope or package with sufficient postage—otherwise, you can kiss your entry form and supporting documents goodbye. (In any case, make sure you retain copies as we cannot guarantee that we won't spill coffee on your materials or lose them altogether.)

Communications About Your Record

We are not able to provide advice about establishing records, nor discuss your chances of having your record published. Once you've sent your entry materials to us, it's up to us to make a decision. We reserve the right to determine, at our sole discretion, whether or not to publish your record. So please—don't call us, we'll call you.

Publisher's Note

We are often asked whether all the records in this book are true. Now that you've read through our documentation procedures, we think you'll agree that it would be difficult to fool us. Because photos can be retouched and witnesses' signatures forged, and because we cannot investigate every submission, we have to rely on the good faith of those who submit records to us. But if we discover that a record you submitted to us is fraudulent, we will prosecute you to the full extent of the law.

THE HUMAN BODY

Worst Memory

Oly Rolvaag of Molde, Norway, constantly forgets things, such as where he's going or what his last name is. Rolvaag has slept in the wrong house, reported to work at the wrong job, and once told a perfect stranger—who he thought was his wife—that he didn't like her hairdo and wished she had left it the way it was.

Greatest Extrasensory Perception

Blossom Wise, a psychic in Ojai, California, has a 98 percent accuracy rate guessing people's names, astrological signs, social security numbers, least favorite vegetables, and the colors of their underwear. Wise has helped local police departments solve 32 kidnapping cases, and she has helped many of her friends find the car keys they've misplaced and the socks they've lost in the laundry.

Best Eyesight

Cece Leclere of Basel, Switzerland, has what scientists call "megavision." She can see through clothing, manila envelopes, curtains, and sometimes even brick walls. People often make her sick, though, because looking at their internal organs nauseates her.

Worst Smelling Armpits

The armpits of Nicolai Glatina from Cluj, Romania, smell so bad that people who stand near him start to gasp, cough, or faint. Glatina bathes and uses underarm deodorant daily and even splashes on handfuls of cologne under his shirt at work, but every few hours the overpowering stench comes back. On the positive side, people always give him plenty of room on the crowded bus he rides to work. Also, he dates a woman who works in a fish market and doesn't think he smells bad at all.

Waxiest Ears

The ears of Lena Wroclaw of Lodz, Poland, produce so much wax, they must be cleaned once a day or she is unable to hear anything. Wroclaw has a five-foot ball of wax collected from her ears over the last six years, which she proudly displays in her living room.

Worst Breath

Tibor Zogu, a dairy farmer in Fieri, Albania, has such bad breath that his farm animals run away when he approaches. Zogu's favorite foods are steamed onions, creamed onions, fried onions, and raw onions. For a treat he likes his onion seasoned with garlic. Zogu, who lives alone, hasn't brushed his teeth in 21 years.

Longest Tongue

Dith Pang from Kampong Thum, Kampuchea (Cambodia), has a tongue that measures 11¾ inches long when fully extended. He talks with his teeth clenched so his tongue won't fall out onto his chest and frighten people. When he was a boy, Pang imitated frogs by catching flies with his long tongue, but his mother found out and made him stop.

Most Unkempt Beard

Ayatollah Salredi of Nehbandan, Iran, has not trimmed his beard since he started growing it 53 years ago. The birds in the neighborhood often make daring dives, attempting either to get some of the food that has accumulated over the years or the insects who make their home in the ayatollah's beard.

Most Broken Bones

Bruce Bracknell of Toowoomba, Australia, is a fruit picker who often goes too far out on a limb. He has smashed his nose, cracked his skull, broken all his ribs, and fractured bones in both arms and legs. Also, during his falls, he has broken the bones of five other people, two dogs, a horse, and his pet koala, Sheila.

Strongest Handshake

A steel-mill worker named Rodney Olatunji from Keetmanshoop, Namibia, is so strong, he no longer shakes hands with anyone for fear of hurting them. Olatunji has injured 18 people while shaking their hands, so now he simply waves or nods to others. When his children misbehave, he lets his wife discipline them. If he spanks them, they might wind up in a hospital.

Cheapest Artificial Heart

Molly Ryan of Ballycastle, Northern Ireland, built a fully functional artificial heart from household items. Ryan fashioned the heart from plastic tubing, cigarette filters, dental floss, and a modified motor from a vacuum cleaner. Though the heart costs only $28.48 to make and has worked for over three years in Ryan's aging dog, Seamas, the medical world has shown no interest.

Greatest Human Guinea Pig

Wattila Thisdou of Sehwan, Pakistan, was paid to donate her body to science for one year. Among other things, she was given 22 experimental drugs, deprived of sleep, tickled for two days, put in a zero-gravity chamber, fed nothing but curried rice for a week, and basted like a turkey while she sat in a sauna. Thisdou made it through the year in perfect health, but became ill when she found out how much of her income the government took in taxes.

Worst Flatulence

Jan Scheldt of Ghent, Belgium, is unrivaled when it comes to volume and pungency in flatulence. He can be heard one hundred yards away when breaking wind. Scheldt's flatulence is so powerful, it often tears holes in his pants.

Longest Umbilical Cord

Khan Nekshan of Ulan Bator, Mongolia, was born with a six-foot, four-inch umbilical cord. His parents were so proud of it, they dried it out, stuffed it, mounted it, and hung it over the fireplace in their living room.

Most Organ Transplants

Liv Johannsen of Uppsala, Sweden, has had her liver, pancreas, spleen, stomach, gall bladder, and small intestines replaced. Her torso has so many operation scars it looks like a road map, but Johannsen is delighted. She can eat anything she wants and never get a stomachache.

Most Painful Sunburn

Adele Blakemore of Winooski, Vermont, wasn't used to getting much sun until she went to Acapulco, Mexico, for vacation. Lulled by the heat of the sun and the sound of the surf, Blakemore fell asleep on the beach in her bikini and woke up in agony later that evening. Her entire body was so badly sunburned that doctors rubbed her with salve and wrapped her from head to toe in surgical gauze. She remained bandaged during her entire three-week stay in Mexico. For next year's vacation, Blakemore is planning a trip to Alaska.

Fastest Weight Gain

Julio Javier of La Paz, Bolivia, claimed his dead mother appeared in a dream one night, telling him that he must eat more than anyone else in his village during the upcoming All

Gluttons Feast. In seven days of feasting, Javier gained 92 pounds. Shortly thereafter, according to Javier, his mother appeared in another dream, telling him to take the extra weight off because he "looked disgusting."

Most Advanced Hearing

Ahmad Abundi of Maradi, Niger, can overhear conversations up to 75 feet away. Abundi was an undercover agent for the Niger government's secret police until this book was published. He is now a gossip columnist for a local paper.

ANIMAL, VEGETABLE, OR MINERAL

Laziest Animal

The potbellied sloth of southwestern Australia sleeps 20 hours a day. During the four hours it is awake, the sloth eats berries and leaves, lies in the sun, and scratches its belly. The sloth is in danger of extinction because mating takes too much energy.

Most Unique Pattern on a Zebra

A zebra in Obbia, Somalia, does not have the typical pattern of stripes associated with its species. Instead, this particular zebra has vertical stripes of various widths that look very much like the bar codes on items found in a supermarket.

Ostrich with Head Buried for Longest Time

An ostrich in Lamu, Kenya, buried its head underground for 21 days. Ostriches bury their heads because they think that if they can't see anything, their predators can't see them. This particular ostrich was so frightened, it corkscrewed its head and neck four feet into the ground. A local construction crew was hired to dig it out.

Fussiest Cat

An Angora cat belonging to King Zahelim of Syria was so spoiled, it would eat only fresh salmon caught in a seaport 150 miles away from its home. The fish had to be cleaned, sprinkled with a touch of lemon juice, and served from a carved golden bowl. One day, the special bowl disappeared and the cat refused to eat. Before the king could find another carved golden bowl, the cat starved to death.

Dumbest Cow

Daisy, a Holstein cow living on a farm near Hazlehurst, Wisconsin, doesn't know where she is going most of the time. That's because she loves to drink milk from the bottom of the milk pails that Ralph Swenson uses on his farm. The trouble is, she can't get her tongue all the way down to the bottom of the pail, and by the time she figures that out, she can't get the pail off her head. Swenson says that he has to pull Daisy's head out of a milk pail several times a week.

Most Annoying Insect

The Mozambique brain bug is a rare but hardy insect that crawls into the ears of sleeping persons and, once inside the head, starts buzzing. Most of its victims go stark raving mad before the brain bug leaves.

Kangaroo with the Biggest Pocket

A female kangaroo in Tumbarumba, Australia, has a pocket that, when stretched to capacity, can hold 245 cubic inches of cargo. The local zoo bought "Karla" from her owner and has trained her to pick up litter around the zoo and put it in her pouch.

Friendliest Giraffe

Morgana, the kissing giraffe, lives in a zoo in Zeist, Netherlands. She greets Hans Apeldorn with a juicy kiss on the nose every morning when he brings her food. Apeldorn's ex-wife grew jealous of his relationship with Morgana and eventually divorced him because he was spending too much time with the giraffe.

Cruelest Guide Dog

Brutus, a former guide dog for the blind in South Bend, Indiana, played vicious tricks on his unfortunate owners. He led blind people into walls, pulled them down flights of stairs, and guided three owners into open manholes in the street. In a case that went to court, he was found guilty of manslaughter and put to sleep.

Most Corrupt Police Dog

A drug-sniffing police dog in the border town of Tijuana, Mexico, was discovered to be on the take for over eight years. The dog allowed dealers who secretly gave him choice cuts of sirloin steak and filet mignon to pass suitcases of drugs over the border.

Dogs' Best Friend

Ollie, an orangutan, loves dogs, and dogs love him right back. Ollie belongs to Dr. Harry Philpott, a veterinarian from Burlingame, California, who taught him to catch lice that live in dog hair. Dr. Philpott even uses Ollie to occasionally remove ticks, fleas, and lice from his own hair.

Most Conniving Canines

Trixie and Dixie are two beguiling basset hounds who love to put people on. Whenever guests arrive at their owners Walla Walla, Washington, home, they try to pretend that they are the longest basset hound in the world...which they would be if they weren't two precocius pups. Their owners have been trying to book Trixie and Dixie on "Late Night with David Letterman," but so far, with no luck.

Rudest Parrot

A parrot in New Orleans, Louisiana, has been taught to insult everyone but her owner. "Putrid Polly," as she is called, spits, scratches, or bites anyone who comes near her. She speaks with a Cajun accent and can curse in either English or French. Polly's favorite remark is "Drop dead, you ugly geek!"

Most Annoying Woodpeckers

The woodpeckers on Monomoy Island, Massachusetts, hammer away all night, keeping all residents awake. As a direct result, the island residents are always tired and cranky. The birth rate and the divorce rate are far above average. The island has a population of 320 people, 16 of whom are psychiatrists.

Best-Mannered Parrot

Patrick is a parrot with good breeding. He belongs to the royal family in Great Britain and was raised by a nanny who insisted that he eat properly—with utensils. Patrick was taught to pick up and eat his birdseed with a spoon. He also wipes his beak with a small napkin when he finishes eating and says "excuse me" after he belches.

Most Dangerous Venus's-Flytrap

There is a Venus's-flytrap in Harbinger, North Carolina, that enjoys eating much more than just insects. Many unlucky admirers of the plant have been unaware that it can lean forward a few feet. The flytrap has taken bites out of numerous ties, buttons, and scarves, and also a few small pets, although it seems to be most fond of bologna sandwiches.

Foulest Smelling Orchid

The Violet Stench orchid is an endangered species found mainly in Florida. Its vivid violet and yellow colors make it an attractive flower, but it smells so bad that it makes bees dizzy and nauseous.

Largest Grown Vegetable

The town of Elbasan, Albania, is proud to be the home of the world's largest cucumber. Eleven inches in circumference and 17 feet long, the cucumber has been bronzed and now serves as a statue outside City Hall.

Most Creative Use of Mashed Potatoes

During a particularly bitter winter in Copeland, Idaho, Marvin Franks found himself in his drafty cabin with a six-month supply of potatoes. He mashed a few hundred, added a little butter and a little plaster, and insulated the interior of his cabin.

Strongest Coffee

The coffee grown in Pôrto Alegre, Brazil, is so strong, just one cup will keep a person awake for 24 hours. If milk or cream is added, however, it lasts only 18 hours.

Toughest Nut to Crack

The shell of the kakanut, which grows in Central Africa, is so tough, it's almost impossible to crack. Everything had been tried: bashing it with a rock, having an elephant stomp on it, even shooting bullets at it. Finally, the shell was split by the particle accelerator at the Sanford Institute of Technology in California, but a scientist who tasted the nutmeat spit it out because it was bitter.

Least Nutritious Breakfast Cereal

Candy Crunchies is a British cold cereal that consists of marshmallow bits covered with icing and sprinkled with confectioner's sugar. It has no vitamins or minerals, one bowl contains eight ounces of sugar, and each box comes with a tube of toothpaste.

Richest Pastry

A pastry shop in Zurich, Switzerland, makes a dessert known as the *schlagshocken*, or "sugar shock" torte. Twelve pounds of cream, sugar, eggs, honey, and chocolate go into each four-inch square of schlagshocken. The Swiss are used to this rich confection, but visitors have passed out from the sugar rush after just one piece. Some have had pimples break out all over their faces within days of eating it.

Most Disgusting Flavor of Ice Cream

Judging by the percentage of people who get sick after their first taste, Chocolate Salmon Surprise is the worst flavor of ice cream. A Hilo, Hawaii, homemade ice cream shop serves the ice cream with a little bucket in case the customer gets ill. The ice cream shop offers no refunds, but reports that most customers eventually try it out of curiosity.

SCIENCE AND TECHNOLOGY

Most Impressive School Science Project

Horace MacIntyre of Albert Einstein High School in Seattle, Washington, won 11 awards for his inventions before he built an antigravity molecular phase shifter for his final science project. MacIntyre used the phase shifter on his teacher, Mabel Simpson, who levitated in front of the classroom and then came back down, hard. MacIntyre received a "B" for the project because his teacher sprained her ankle when she landed.

Most Effective Optical Illusion

The Leaning Tower of Pisa in Italy is a centuries-old optical illusion. Scientists have recently discovered that the Leaning Tower actually is not leaning at all. It only appears to lean because the whole street and nearby buildings are built on a slant.

Most Durable Nail Polish

Technoid Industries of El Segundo, California, has invented a nail polish made of liquid titanium, the metal that helps prevent reentering spacecraft from burning up. The nail polish, which comes in jet black and gun-metal gray, will not chip, peel, or crack and can withstand heat up to 3,500 degrees Fahrenheit. However, once the nail polish is put on, it can be removed only by a laser beam.

Longest Pending Patent

The family of Jeffrey Kosro, a nineteenth-century American inventor who died penniless, has had a patent pending since 1883. Kosro's invention was a small, circular, barbed-wire fence designed to prevent dogs from urinating on fire hydrants. It worked but was never used because too many buildings in the town where it was tested burned to the ground while firefighters gingerly tried to hook up their hoses to the hydrants through the barbed wire.

Most Versatile Robot

Nippon Artificial Intelligence Inc. in Tokyo, Japan, has built a robot that can speak Japanese and English. The robot, affectionately called "Hai-Tek," can also vacuum, dust, answer the door or phone, mow the lawn, and do many other household chores. Hai-Tek can play chess and backgammon, balance a checkbook, and even bake a cake. Hai-Tek has been spending its spare time at a nearby auto plant assembly line since it has fallen in love with a welding robot.

Greatest Amount of Liposuction

After having 84 pounds removed by liposuction, Gabrielle Grossman of Montreux, Switzerland, weighed 108 pounds and later won the Miss Montreux Beauty Pageant. Unfortunately, on the day of the pageant it was cold and windy. Without all the fat she normally had as insulation, Grossman caught pneumonia and died shortly after being crowned.

Biggest Mix-Up in a Hospital

Caroline Carnes checked into a hospital in the Seychelles to have her appendix removed, but the staff confused her with another patient and sent her to the mental ward where no one believed her when she insisted she was in the wrong place. Carnes spent three days in a straitjacket before the confusion was finally cleared up. She was quickly brought to the right operating room, but her chart was misplaced and the doctor removed her large intestine. She found out about the mix-up two months later when her appendix started hurting again.

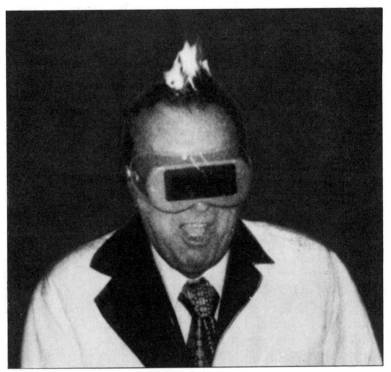

Most Durable Wig

Harry Drummond, a chemist in Oxford, Mississippi, invented a wig made from a blend of human hair, vulcanized rubber, and asbestos. It is so durable, it can be set on fire and extinguished and will still look great. The hair is guaranteed not to fall out or change color.

Worst-Tasting Cold Remedy

A 93-year-old gypsy who lives in Yecla, Spain, is reputed to have amazing healing powers. Isabella Azura prepares a special "soup" to cure colds. It is made with seaweed, bitter olives, jalapeño peppers, and eels. Some parents save the leftover soup and make their children drink it when they misbehave.

Most Childproof Aspirin Bottle

A Chinese pharmaceutical firm, Kunming Corp., has invented an aspirin bottle that is also a puzzle. The cap has 13 moving parts and requires 39 moves before it can be opened. To make it even safer, the company produces a new cap every six months. Ironically, the biggest market for Kunming's aspirin are children who buy it to see if they can solve the puzzle.

ARTISTIC ACHIEVEMENTS

Nosiest Photographer

Rudolfo Spaggiari was the nosiest, most persistent photographer ever known. Covering scandals, rumors, and celebrities' private lives in Rome, Italy, Spaggiari was often attacked by celebrities whose pictures he was trying to take. He was not afraid to hide in people's cars or follow them into restrooms. He snapped his final picture just before he was pushed off a balcony outside a well-known movie star's bedroom.

Happiest Artist

Li Fung Lu of Beijing, China, was once the world's happiest artist. All his works were portraits of himself laughing hysterically. Li stopped laughing, however, when he was jailed by the Chinese police for his avant-garde approach to art. Now he works 12 hours a day breaking rocks and is no longer the world's happiest artist.

Largest Painting

Artist Josef Szubin of Brzeg, Poland, thinks big. Currently, he is working on a realistic painting of the wall of a prison in his hometown. His canvas measures 100-feet tall by 50-feet wide. It's about the same size as the wall he's copying. The canvas was donated to him by the prisoners, who hope to become famous when Szubin's work is finished.

Youngest Artist to Have Own Art Show

Martina Comstock, daughter of famous artist Garth Comstock, of New York, had her first art exhibition at the age of four. Garth rented a gallery and hung 16 of Martina's best finger paintings. All 16 sold for $500 apiece, and the president of a fine arts college offered Martina a scholarship to cover the costs of tuition, art supplies, and nanny.

Greatest Forgery

British painter and art historian Alexander Adams claimed he found six paintings by renowned Renaissance painter Tintoretto. Experts from all over the world confirmed the paintings' authenticity, and Adams sold them all for $6.1 million. Seven years later, it was discovered that on the back of one of the canvasses was written "Norby's Art Supplies, London W1." Adams admitted forging the six paintings. He is now in jail, teaching art to the other inmates.

Grossest National Product

Art is one of the major exports of Belize, a small country in Central America. Many of its people create unique murals by pasting dead insects onto cardboard. These "bug murals" are exported to Surinam in South America, where people feed them to their pet iguanas.

Most Unflattering Statue

Iain Llangelfni, five-time mayor of Caernarvon, Wales, hired respected sculptor Brent Monmouth to create a statue of him. At the time, Monmouth had recently stopped doing realistic art and had started working in the cubist tradition of Pablo Picasso. It was a great surprise to the whole town when the statue was unveiled at City Hall. Llangelfni's head was a triangle, his ears were shaped like hot dog buns, and both of his eyes were on the left side of his face.

Costliest Unproduced Screenplay

Top-notch New York novelist-screenwriter William Golden was paid $1 million to write a movie for Global Films. The executives claimed that the script, about the life of Abraham Lincoln, was "perfect" and gave Golden another $150,000 to do a minimal rewrite. For the third draft, the executives insisted that he change Lincoln's assassination because it was "too depressing." Golden told them to drop dead, the studio chief was later fired, and the picture was never made.

Most Egotistical Film Star

French film star Yves Monet will not work on any film without a manager, hairdresser, fashion consultant, chauffeur, bodyguard, and astrologer of his own. He drinks only Dom Perignon champagne while on the set. Monet has said he had many of his directors fired because "they did not make me look as attractive as I really am."

Most Effective TV Commercial

An exterminator in Newark, New Jersey, ran a 30-second TV commercial for one week and received over 12,000 calls from potential customers before he was thrown in jail. The exterminator illegally inserted a subliminal message into the commercial that read: "Let us exterminate your cockroaches before they exterminate you."

Most Ridiculous Plea for Money by a TV Evangelist

Reverend Luther Bob Braithwaite told a local TV audience in Clarksville, Arkansas, that he desperately needed $25,000 in order to buy two more TV cameras and some new suits and to hire a makeup artist. Reverend Braithwaite fell to his knees, burst into tears, and wildly pulled at his hair, wailing that a voice had told him the night before that he needed to look better on camera.

Most Undeserved Oscar Award

Benny Glickman received an Academy Award for special effects on the film *Galactic Terrorists*. Benny's father, Sy Glickman, was head of the special effects unit and got his son listed in the film's credits, even though the 18-year-old high school dropout did nothing more than bring the crew sandwiches and coffee.

Most Repulsive TV Commercial Jingle

The Johnson Tire Company owns a chain of tire stores in Ohio. They produced a 30-second TV commercial that ended with a jingle sung by men in deep, threatening voices. The lyrics were:

Buy Johnson tires.
Use your head.
If you buy someone else's,
You're as good as dead.

Longest Death Scene

Aging Dutch actress Marika Arnhem took 14 minutes to die after being stabbed by another actor in a play. Her death scene was supposed to take only 20 seconds but, as it was the final performance of her career, Arnhem took advantage of the opportunity to bid her fans a long farewell.

Cruelest Theater Critic

Clive Stickney, theater critic for a newspaper in Bristol, England, has caused scores of insecure actors to retire from the stage. Several have attempted suicide after reading his vicious reviews. Stickney once claimed an actress had "the facial expressions of a punch-drunk boxer, a voice like a kazoo, and the grace of a three-legged cow." Stickney, who only reviews shows he despises, once wrote that a certain playwright "should be burned at the stake along with all copies of his plays."

Strangest Shakespeare Production

The drama department of Osceola Junior College in Osceola, Iowa, staged a bizarre version of William Shakespeare's *Julius Caesar*. The play was set in and around a 1920s Chicago meat-packing plant. The actors wore butcher's aprons instead of togas and, in place of swords, dueled with cattle prods and meat cleavers.

Rudest Theatergoer

Constantine Petrakis of Corfu, Greece, boos actors in plays he does not like. During some performances, he has gotten into shouting matches with actors, directors, theater managers, and other audience members. Petrakis once threw one of his shoes at a lead actor he said was "hamming it up."

Most Annoying Street Mime

Maury Parks, a street mime in Pittsburgh, Pennsylvania, imitates people who walk by him. He follows individuals until they're embarrassed enough to give him money or until they threaten to hurt him. On days when nobody seems to notice him performing, Parks occasionally sticks out a leg and trips people, hoping to gather a crowd.

Least Helpful Advice Column

Nettie Christensen has an advice column in the Corvallis (Oregon) *Beacon* called "You Need Help!" Some of Christensen's worst advice includes telling a woman to divorce her husband because he snored and counseling a 15-year-old girl to run away from home because her parents wouldn't let her wear makeup.

Most Pointless U.N. Speech

After many years of trying, the tiny African country of Selotho was finally admitted to the United Nations. But in his first speech, the Selothon representative cursed the U.N. for taking so long to admit his country, calling them "argumentative asses who never accomplish anything." The U.N. immediately voted unanimously to throw Selotho out, and the representative was deported.

Stupidest Lyrics to a National Anthem

The anthem for the Republic of Maldives translates as follows:

Maldives, where nothing happens.
No murder, coups, or snow.
We'll stay until we move or die.
Maldives, we love you so.

Loudest Opera Singer

Giulio Lagomarsino, an opera singer in Naples, Italy, has sung notes that reached a level of 105 decibels. Lagomarsino's voice, which has shattered opera house light bulbs and the eyeglasses of some patrons, has even short-circuited the hearing aids of a few elderly audience members.

Most-Loved Opera Star

Giuseppe Blanco, an opera star from Milan, Italy, was so popular that women would break into his house to be with him. One night, three of his most ardent admirers met outside his door and argued about who loved him the most. When Blanco came home, they demanded to know which of them he most loved. Blanco refused to answer, saying he liked them equally. Infuriated, the three fans burned his house down. Blanco moved away, and he never sang again.

Dumbest Opera

The Crazy Shoemaker, by Italian composer Giacomo Capiletti, was performed just once in 1783. It tells the story of an ugly shoemaker who falls in love with a beautiful princess while fitting her for a pair of dancing shoes. When the shoemaker tells the princess of his love for her, she laughs in his face and says she is marrying a prince. Heartbroken, the shoemaker gets his revenge by making a special pair of boots and sending them to the prince. The prince is delighted by the gift, but soon finds that he cannot remove the exquisitely-crafted boots, which are cutting off the circulation in his legs. Forced to choose between life with the boots on or his legs off, the prince loses his mind and is sent to an insane asylum. The princess, learning what has happened, goes wild with rage and beats the little shoemaker to death with her dancing shoes. The princess then takes her own life, the king has a heart attack, and the country is overrun by socialists.

Most Obnoxious Musician

Ernst Offenbach is a one-man, 17-instrument, marching band. He marches the main street of Friedrichskoog, West Germany, loudly blowing, ringing, whistling, or drumming at pedestrians and following them until they give him a donation. He tells them that he is saving money for music lessons.

Most Out-of-Control Orchestra

The musicians in the symphony orchestra of Minsk in the USSR feud with one another: the Marxist-Leninists hate the Stalinists; the Armenians hate the White Russians; the atheists hate the Russian Orthodox; and the tympanist hates the second violinist, who he recently broke up with. The angry musicians play at different volumes, in different tempos, and in different keys. The last three conductors left for positions in lesser-known orchestras to preserve their mental health.

Most Sensitive Violinist

Dragutin Cevik of Zagreb, Yugoslavia, plays violin with such feeling that his audiences are moved to tears. On occasion he has stopped playing in the middle of a solo to wipe away his own tears and blow his nose. Cevik is extremely sensitive to noise, refusing to perform if any audience members cough during his performance.

Longest Time on Air by a DJ

Los Angeles disc jockey Bill Ratner bet the owner of the easy-listening station where he worked $50,000 that he could stay on the air 14 days in a row without sleep. With just 12 hours to go, Ratner snapped, locking himself in the on-air studio, playing Christmas carols over and over at the wrong speed, and screaming into the microphone stories about how he was mistreated and ignored as a boy. The station owner let Ratner mumble incoherently until he reached the record because over four million people were listening, and most of them wanted Ratner to win the bet.

Most Insulting Radio Talk Show Host

Rick Rudman is the long-time host of the "Shut Up and Listen" radio show, broadcast from Pierre, South Dakota. Rudman prides himself on insulting each guest. He has called an Olympic gold-medal gymnast "a hard-core steroid junkie," a nun working with the homeless "a con artist with a guilty conscience," and the author of a book on cholesterol "a walking, talking vegetable who should be ground into hamburger meat."

Most Repulsive Punk Rock Group

Raw Sewage, a punk band that hails from Key West, Florida, pours buckets of sewage on their audiences. While Raw Sewage performs, driver education films of horrible car crashes are projected on a screen behind them.

Most Unappreciated Band

On the island of Madagascar lives a strange group of musicians who play high-pitched dog whistles. Although dogs love their music, humans can't hear a thing and ignore the musicians when they're performing.

Phoniest Blind Blues Singer

Charles "Blind Man" Bluff of Buhl, Alabama, was born with normal eyesight to a middle-class family. However, he wanted to suffer and sing the blues. He left home to live in a cold, dark shack; bought a Seeing Eye dog, dark glasses, and a tin cup; and supported himself by playing guitar and singing on street corners. Bluff almost starved to death until he identified a pickpocket in a police lineup and began a high-paying career as a police informant.

Worst Public Behavior by a Rock Group

A British rock group called Demented Weasels went on a rampage in the Hotel Paddington in Croydon, England. They smashed everything in their rooms, spray-painted obscenities on other hotel room doors, and destroyed a grand piano in the main lounge. At their trial, the Demented Weasels testified that they were upset because mints had not been left on their hotel room pillows.

Bluest Blues Musician

"Whining" Willie Huxley of Pea Ridge, Arkansas, lives alone, rarely goes out, and refuses to answer his doorbell or telephone. Willie had a hit with his first blues record, "Bluer Than You," but the record company and its attornies cheated him out of most of the profits. Since then, Willie has been too depressed to write any more songs.

Worst Circus Knife Thrower

Rick Tyler was the knife thrower for a small circus in Calgary, Alberta. He nicked, cut, or seriously injured 14 female assistants, one of whom angrily threw knives back at him. He can no longer find willing assistants and has retired.

Most Dangerous Magician

Esmerelda was an extremely forgetful Portuguese magician. She performed illusions in which volunteers from the audience would seem to disappear into thin air. The problem was, after they disappeared, she sometimes couldn't find them. Her career ended tragically when she sawed a small boy in half and then could not remember how to put the two halves back together again.

Most Daring Juggler

Vance Grillo of Venice, California, has successfully juggled a running chainsaw, a live hand grenade, and a loaded Uzi submachine gun for more than 50 performances without ever causing a fatality. He does, however, fire warning shots in the air at times to quiet hecklers or to encourage wild applause.

Most Unusual Circus

The county fair in Pulaski, Virginia, can claim some very original acts: hogs that jump through a ring of fire, a bareback rider who leaps from one cow to another, roosters that perform on a trapeze five feet off the ground, and a lamb that is shot out of a cannon and caught by two farmers.

BUILDINGS, STRUCTURES, AND LOCATIONS

Flimsiest House

In the Sahara Desert some nomadic tribes construct houses made of camel dung and chicken wire. The houses are so light they can be strapped on a camel's back and carried to the next location.

Most Haunted House

The Quarry House in Macroom, Ireland, has, according to ten expert parapsychologists, five ghosts haunting it. Doors and windows regularly fly open and slam shut, and food and silverware fly around the kitchen. Footsteps, crying, and cackling laughter can also be heard in the uninhabited house. Sometimes, when a visitor is about to sit on a chair, the chair mysteriously moves and the person falls on the floor.

Stickiest Floor in a Movie Theater

The cement floor of the Rialto Theater in Boron, California, has not been cleaned in seven years. It is so sticky from candy, gum, and spilled soft drinks that many theatergoers cannot lift their shoes from the tacky floor without using the crowbar supplied under every seat.

Most Luxurious Prison

The Paradise Correctional Facility near Las Vegas, Nevada, is a little-known, minimum-security prison for white-collar criminals. Various stock brokers, politicians, celebrities, and high-ranking intelligence and military officers have served time there. Each private-cell suite features a bedroom, dining room, den, bath, TV, VCR, sauna, and daily maid service. Prisoners are allowed weekend guests and one two-week vacation each year.

Fanciest Swimming Pool

Armando Bracco, a financier in San Diego, California, has a custom-built swimming pool that encircles his home like a moat. The sides of the pool are decorated with jade and mother-of-pearl, spelling out "Armando" all the way around. The pool has a wide array of colorful underwater lights and is surrounded by barbed wire to keep out uninvited guests.

Least Comfortable Furniture

In Madras, India, a small company makes furniture exclusively for Hindu holy men. All their chairs, desks, couches, beds, and toilet seats are covered with nails.

Friendliest Cemetery

The owner of a cemetery in Velp, Netherlands, goes out of his way to cheer up visitors. He puts out fresh tulips every week; serves free Dutch cocoa, cookies, and cheese; and employs a small brass band to stroll the grounds daily, playing happy tunes.

Least Attractive Highway Observation Point

In the industrial center of Romania, near the town of Slatina, there is an observation area off the highway where travelers can rest and look out over the countryside. The outpost overlooks an automobile junkyard, a steel mill that discharges huge clouds of smoke, and an enormous open-pit coal mine. A telescope at the observation area is free to the public, but most visitors stay in their cars because the air is difficult to breathe.

Tallest Mailbox

Lee Patterson of Bozeman, Montana, has a 14-foot-tall mailbox outside his home. It doesn't pose a problem for Lee, who plays center for a local basketball team and likes to jump to get his mail. His mailman, though, has to stand on top of his mail truck to reach the box.

Most Dangerous Road

The Via Crespi in Milan, Italy, nicknamed "Blood Boulevard," has no speed limit, and the only sign visible lists the number of traffic fatalities that have occurred in that location (112 at last count). Sports cars have been clocked at over 140 miles per hour, sidewalks are used as passing lanes, and fast-moving cars often ram slower cars out of their way.

Most Poorly Maintained Highway

The major highway south of Dakar, Senegal, is in such terrible condition that most drivers go miles out of their way to avoid it. There are no lines left indicating lanes on the road, and all the exit signs have fallen down. The road's potholes are larger than most compact cars. Many people who drive the highway are never seen again.

Most Distracting Billboard

The Salonika Corp. in Athens, Greece, set up a billboard that featured a moving hologram (3-D light projection) of a popular belly dancer. Fourteen auto accidents occurred in just two days after the billboard was put up, so Salonika was ordered to take it down.

Filthiest Beach

A one-mile stretch of beach in the Gulf of Oman is so dirty, people don't come near it. Underground oil has seeped up into the sand, trapping paper and plastic products that have been littered there. A developer has plans to turn it into "the world's most picturesque garbage dump."

Biggest Mirage

About half the people who visit El Mirage, Arizona, claim they can see a magnificent city of towering glass skyscrapers. The other half say all they can see are desert sand and another tourist trap that costs $2.50 per person.

Slowest Quicksand

The quicksand in the jungle of the Sudan near Malakal is lethal but particularly slow. Animals and humans cannot escape once they've stepped into it, but it takes a good two to three hours before the victim is completely submerged. Ali Hamadi, a Sudanese ecologist, had a pencil and a piece of paper with him when he stepped into the Malakal quicksand. He was able to write out his will, fold it into a paper airplane, and fly it to safety, before he was sucked under.

Ugliest Rainbows

In Newcastle, England, the mines send tons of coal dust into the air. The sky is so thick with soot particles that often after a rain the only colors visible in a rainbow are smudgy black, brown, and gray.

MECHANICAL INVENTIONS

Noisiest Ambulance

An ambulance in Eau Claire, Wisconsin, had such a loud siren, the effect bordered on pain. Drivers let go of their steering wheels and covered their ears when it drove by, causing minor accidents. Now the ambulance driver just honks the horn.

Noisiest Subway Train

A subway train in Warsaw, Poland, is so old, it wobbles down the track shooting sparks and grinding metal at a level of 135 decibels. Most people unfortunate enough to have to ride this train either wear earplugs they've brought or desperately cover their ears with their hands. Children like to ride it because they can scream at the top of their lungs and no one will tell them to be quiet.

Greatest Fuel Economy

Otto Kessler of Stuttgart, West Germany, designed a two-seater car that could get up to 132 miles per gallon. But his car didn't use gasoline. It ran on Liebfraumilch, a German white wine that costs considerably more than gas, so no one was interested in manufacturing Kessler's car.

Most Extravagant Limousine

Conspicuous Carsumption Ltd. of Beverly Hills, California, rents a special one-of-a-kind Cadillac limousine. The limo, which costs $1,000 per hour, seats 12 and has a small satellite dish on the roof, large-screen TV, VCR, full bar, refrigerator, freezer, microwave oven, pinball machine, personal computer, library, and telescope. Also, the roof slides back and the seats fold up to accommodate a hideaway hot tub.

Brightest Traffic Light

In Wheeler Park, Nevada, the traffic signal on the main street was illuminated by an experimental laser beam. The red, yellow, and green lights could be seen a mile away at night. The new light proved impractical, however, because drivers couldn't look at it unless they were wearing sunglasses.

Biggest Traffic Jam

After a World Cup soccer victory by the Spanish team, the city of Madrid was tied up in a 24-hour traffic jam. The police had been so happy about the victory, they all took a day off from work.

Most Dangerous Machine

The high-speed, automatic shrink wrap machine at Auto-Wrap Industries in Cedar City, Utah, is very difficult to operate. Six months of study and a year of apprenticeship are required before operators can manage it alone. Even so, five workers have been accidently caught up in the machine and wrapped in brightly colored plastic.

Most Unpleasant Carousel

The carousel in Runanga, New Guinea, isn't a very fun ride. Riders sit on human skeletons instead of wooden horses. Instead of caliope music, a local band bangs drums and emits shrill war cries.

Most Powerful Pipe Organ

The First Adventist Colonial Church in Bienvenue, French Guiana, has a magnificent 3,000-pipe organ. The vibrations from the organ are so powerful, they shake the church's floorboards. The pastor often signals the organist to play loud and scary music when he feels someone is not being honest during confession.

Most Powerful Vacuum Cleaner

The Vaculite Corp. of Urbana, Illinois, built an industrial vacuum cleaner, the SUC-5000, that has so much suction it can pull wallpaper off of walls. Those who buy the vacuum are cautioned not to wear jewelry, or neckties, or loose-fitting clothes while operating it.

Digital Watch with the Most Functions

Tempus Fugit Inc. of Sheffield, England, has invented a digital watch with 87 functions. In addition to telling the year, month, day, hour, second, and times around the world, it has an alarm, stop watch, calculator, smoke detector, bottle opener, and air quality analyzer. It can also read body temperature, alcohol/blood level, and pulse rate.

Most Unpredictable Escalator

Kushner's department store in Norwich, Connecticut, has been sued many times because one of their escalators doesn't work properly. At times the escalator will stop completely or reverse direction, throwing shoppers down the mechanical stairs. Now, anyone who rides the escalators has to sign a liability waiver agreement. But all the fuss has provided booming business for Kushner's. They now charge admission for escalator rides. Most of the takers are kids who gather at Kushner's after school looking for some fun and excitement.

Most Locks on an Apartment Door

Alicia Schaefer of Brooklyn, New York, was burglarized three times, so she hired a locksmith to install 21 locks on her door. She has had no burglaries since the locks were put in, but it takes her an average of 12 minutes, 45 seconds to get into her apartment and 10 minutes, 22 seconds to get out.

Most Dangerous Elevator Doors

The elevator doors in a hospital in Pueblo, Colorado, sometimes quickly snap closed with great force, resulting in serious injuries, including broken bones. Many suspect the elevator is rigged to create more patients for the hospital's overstaffed surgical ward.

Least Popular Doll

For a short while, a Swedish company marketed a doll called "Miserable Margrit." She wet her diapers, threw up, cried, and kicked her arms and legs angrily. Margrit, whose face always frowned, also talked when a ring in her back was pulled. She said such phrases as "Shut up," "Get lost," "I hate you," and "I'm telling Mom."

Fastest Hair Dryer

The hair dryers in the Quik Dry Beauty Salon in Hong Kong use the latest microwave technology. An average woman's head of wet hair can be dried thoroughly in 90 seconds. But the hairdresser must be careful to remove all hair curlers and bobby pins, which can explode or melt when the microwave hair dryer is turned on.

BUSINESS AND COMMERCE

Least Reliable Airline

Trans Indonesia Airways has a fleet of six light planes that fly the islands of Southeast Asia. Flights are often delayed hours, sometimes days, when any of the airline's six pilots are sick or simply not in the mood to fly. The friendly pilots often make unannounced stops at various islands to say hello to friends and relatives or just to go fishing.

Stiffest Library Fines

A library in Johnstown, Pennsylvania, is very strict about overdue books. The fine is one dollar per book per day. If a book is not returned before the fine exceeds the cost of replacing it, the Johnstown library calls the borrower's employer and arranges for the fine plus a 25 percent penalty to be taken out of the borrower's next paycheck.

Smallest Ransom for a Kidnapping

Terrorists kidnapped the six-year-old son of the mayor of Tadmor, Syria. The mayor, however, refused to pay the ransom, claiming that the boy always misbehaved and that being kidnapped would teach him a lesson. After a number of threats, the terrorists lowered their ransom demands and finally returned the boy for the equivalent of 50 cents and the mayor's promise not to prosecute them.

Biggest Mistaken Demolition

A Japanese real estate development company built 150 homes in the hills near Ypsilanti, Michigan. The head of the company, who spoke no English, saw the finished houses and told his translator that the dirt surrounding the houses needed to be level. The translator, who spoke little English, told the head of the building contractors that all the houses "needed to be leveled." The contractors, confused but paid by the hour, bulldozed all 150 houses.

Weirdest Bingo Parlor

In Rimbo, Sweden, a barn has been converted into a 440-seat bingo parlor. The game played there is the same as bingo except it is called "Rimbo." When someone wins, the winner is carried around on the shoulders of the other players and everyone shouts "Rimbo" over and over. Winners do not receive any money, but they are given a bottle of buttermilk to take home.

Slowest Fast-Food Restaurant

A fast-food restaurant in Valparaíso, Chile, is run by two brothers who are 92 and 88 years old. One works while the other takes a nap; then they switch. They move so slowly that a sandwich or an order of french fries takes 45 minutes to prepare, and even a soft drink requires a 15-minute wait.

Broadway Producer with the Most Flops

Ronald Gump, a New York real estate tycoon, has had 16 straight flops in 29 years of Broadway stage productions. His biggest bombs include: "Lee!" a musical about Lee Harvey Oswald and the assassination of President John F. Kennedy; "Gridiron Follies," a song-and-dance extravaganza about a group of aging pro football greats who decide they want to be dancers; and "Trash Day," a realistic drama about a seemingly happy family torn apart by arguments about whose turn it is to take out the garbage.

Largest Court Award for a Palimony Case

In Hollywood, California, multimillionaire television producer Albert Spiegel went to court after breaking up with his girlfriend of four years, Candy Bailey. The judge awarded Bailey $600,000 a year until she married, Spiegel's Malibu home, a $50,000-a-year clothes and cosmetics allowance, two of Spiegel's cars, and $20,000 a year for psychiatric counseling to help her cope with the anguish of their separation.

Largest Publishing Advance for the Worst Book

Janice Cartier, whose glitzy, show business novels have made her a multimillionaire, was paid an advance of $8.5 million before writing one word of her latest book, *Sleaze*. The book is about a woman who becomes romantically involved with rock stars, movie stars, TV soap opera stars, and politicians, and then becomes a famous writer after she publishes a book about her experiences. Critics called it the "trashiest of all trash novels," but the book climbed to number one on the *New York Times* bestseller list just one week after it was released.

Most Painful Reward

Parviz Mahin, a janitor in a bus depot in Ankara, Turkey, found and returned a bag of precious stones worth $7.3 million. The jeweler to whom the stones belonged thanked Mahin wholeheartedly but did not offer him even a small reward. When Mahin suggested a small diamond ring for his wife, the jeweler refused. Mahin took a ring angrily and left. He was arrested that evening and sentenced to six years in jail.

Most Bequests in a Will

A philanthropist who died in Mahdia, Tunisia, left a 67-page will, dividing his belongings among his wife, nine children, 13 grandchildren, uncles, aunts, nieces, nephews, business associates, friends, doctor, mailman, secretary, and his pets. No one has received a penny yet, because his barber and gardener have contested the will, saying they deserve a share too.

Greatest Personal Debt

The former treasurer of Paraguay, Pedro Felipe Morales, embezzled money from his country's treasury for 12 years to pay for his expensive taste in women, cars, food, travel, and resort condominiums. When Morales was finally caught, he owed his country $911 million. He was sentenced to 650 years in jail, with no chance for parole until the 400th year.

Most Tax Deductions

Steven Berry, partner in the Los Angeles accounting firm of Berry and Hyde, made $192,500 last year and paid only $409 in taxes. Every time he went to a movie, play, or sporting event, Berry approached strangers, gave them his business card, and legally deducted the cost of the evening as a business expense.

Greatest Welfare Fraud

Dee Cromer of Coventry, England, was at one point receiving the equivalent of $13,200 per month in welfare payments. Using three different names, she was sent money for a total of 17 children, five grandparents, six parents, and three ailing husbands. Cromer, who lived alone, had convinced friends and neighbors to pose as her relatives when social workers came to interview her.

Most-Overpriced Antique

A tin spitoon that Confederate General Robert E. Lee was reputed to have spit into just before surrendering to General Ulysses S. Grant was sold for $3.7 million at the exclusive Shoreham auction studios in London, England. It was later discovered that not Lee but one of his lieutenants had spit into it, but Shoreham refused to take the spitoon back and return the buyer's money.

Worst Use of Money Won in a Lottery

Kenny Carter of Tenafly, New Jersey, won $670,000 in a lottery. He made huge bets with the money in baseball pools, continually losing until the season ended and all he had left was $3,000. His infuriated wife took the remaining $3,000, burned his treasured baseball card collection, and left.

Dumbest April Fool's Joke

Angus McDonald, of Johannesburg, South Africa, is a compulsive practical joker who went a bit too far one April Fool's Day. McDonald, a lookout man for an explosives delivery company, hid his head inside an oversized uniform while sitting in his lookout seat. To the casual observer, it looked as though he'd lost his head—a clever practical joke. But when the story was picked up by a newswire service, McDonald was reprimanded by his boss and then fired from his job.

Most Romantic Drive-In Movie Theater

The Luxury Drive-In in Alamogordo, New Mexico, shows only romantic movies. A red rose is attached to each car speaker. Inexpensive champagne, flowers, and boxes of chocolates are available at the snack bar, which is occasionally used as a wedding chapel. A violinist strolls from car to car each night playing requests.

Most Exclusive Health Club

The Elite Health and Fitness Center in Dallas, Texas, admits only oil executives who earn $100,000 or more a year. Annual membership is $4,800, which does not include valet parking. Members can be expelled from the club for wearing dirty, wrinkled, or unfashionable gym clothes.

Most Boring Cruise Ship

The *S.S. Luzon* is a small cruise ship that sails from Taiwan to the Philippines and back again. The only entertainment the ship provides is a pack of playing cards in each cabin. Fights have broken out among bored, frustrated passengers, and people have been thrown overboard just to break the monotony.

Most Boring Museum

Rutland, Vermont, is the site of the International Lint Museum. This unique museum has displays of lint from such diverse sources as clothing pockets, belly buttons, dryer vents, and screen windows. The museum is free and open to the public six days a week, but it has had only 14 visitors since it opened in 1947.

Least Professional Pharmacy

A pharmacy in Raleigh, North Carolina, sells people drugs without prescriptions as long as the people "have honest faces." The pharmacist, Dr. Ted Whittier, samples every drug before he sells it to make sure of its quality.

Most Unusual Auction

Six families got into a bidding war for a human heart at a hospital in Johannesburg, South Africa. The heart, which was urgently needed for two different heart transplant operations, was auctioned for $125,000. In a gesture of sympathy, the donor's family gave the losing bidder a free liver.

Most Artistic Undertaker

Harlan Pace runs the Serenity Funeral Home in Tempe, Arizona. Pace personally grooms each corpse and selects its clothing and the material to line the coffin, making sure the fabrics are complementary. Pace is a four-time winner of the funeral business' prestigious Golden Casket Award.

Happiest Grave Digger

Pat McGunnagle volunteers at a cemetery in Tullow, Ireland, digging graves in his spare time. McGunnagle loves his work—he's been doing it for 32 years—and he's always in a good mood. Every once in a while a bereaved relative watching the burial of a loved one becomes extremely upset because McGunnagle unconsciously whistles while he works.

Artists' Manager with the Worst Clients

Esther Kilgallen of Rahway, New Jersey, manages 17 different performers, none of whom made more than $750 last year. Some of the talent Kilgallen manages includes a one-armed juggler, a woman who does bird calls while gargling, and a man who blows bubbles from the tip of his tongue and catches them on the tip of his nose.

Rudest Taxi Driver

Agamemnon Carabatsos, a taxi driver on Cyprus, hates the tourists he drives around the island. He refuses to answer their questions, blows cigar smoke in their faces, and throws out anyone who complains about his driving. When people don't tip him, Carabatsos drives off with their luggage.

Worst Lumberjack

Luke Watkins of Banff, Alberta, loves to chop down large trees, but he never knows where they're going to fall. Luke has partially or completely destroyed 15 homes, 9 cars (including two of his own), 5 sets of patio furniture, 11 swing sets, and 22 dog houses.

Shortest Tailor

Mustafa Kamil, a tailor in Isnik, Turkey, is three feet, eight inches tall. He stands on a step ladder to measure his customers for suits. Kamil claims his size is an advantage: he has no trouble threading a needle because his hands are so small, and he can stand between a customer's legs while measuring an inseam.

Stupidest Recycling Project

The city of Kulang, China, has for years been recycling toothpicks. People rummage through garbage pails looking for toothpicks, wash them off, check for splinters, and then take them to one of seven recycling centers. They are paid the equivalent of 35 U.S. cents per pound of reusable toothpicks.

Most Effective Bait

The Bureau of Fishing and Hatcheries in Rekjavik, Iceland, developed a new form of bait that replicates the scent tunas give off when mating. It was highly effective when tested underwater and would have been recommended for widespread use by Iceland's fishing industry had its pungent aroma not attracted a pack of hungry cats to the Bureau's office, completely disrupting the BFH's normal operations.

LIFE-STYLES

Most Accidental Riot

When a new warden took over the State Penitentiary at Athens, Georgia, all the inmates gathered to hear him speak. The warden said in part, "Although you are criminals, I believe you're still entitled to some rights." Unfortunately, his southern drawl made it sound like "some riots," and the inmates tore the prison apart for the next six hours.

Stupidest Protest Group

There is a 14-member organization headquartered in Wellington, New Zealand, that protests the murder of houseflies. They have staged demonstrations in front of pesticide factories and pushed for legislation to make the maximum penalty for killing a fly $2,000 and two weeks in jail. They have failed but are now trying to make it a misdemeanor to possess a flyswatter.

Strangest Bible

A religious cult in Rancho Cordova, California, the Vegetarianists, has printed its own version of the Bible. The Vegetarianist Bible states that God can be found only by eating fresh vegetables. The Bible has black and white photographs of fruits and vegetables, and the first chapter states that human beings evolved from the seeds of a single tomato plant.

Oldest Memo

Archaelogists have finally decoded the earliest petroglyphs found in Mesopotamia. The message they found on the walls of a cave said, "I had to go to the well. Tell Mugwa to watch the fire."

Toughest Driving Test

In Buenos Aires, Argentina, so many people are arrested for drunk driving each year that the Department of

Motor Vehicles has begun issuing licenses only to people who pass a drunk-driving test. Drivers are asked to drive along a crooked line after quickly drinking two 12-ounce bottles of beer.

Least Organized Crime

A group of inexperienced robbers tried several times to rob a bank in Ostend, Belgium. The first time, they arrived on a holiday and the bank was closed. The second time, someone in the bank recognized one of the robbers and said "hello," so they all immediately left. After two more failed attempts, they got out of the bank with a large amount of money. But they had parked in a no-parking zone, and a policeman was writing them a ticket just as they came running up to the car.

Leather Jacket with the Most Zippers

Monty Aylsworth, a clothes designer from Montclair, New Jersey, has designed his own leather jacket. It has 89 zippered pockets, inside and out, including pockets in the middle of the back and under the armpits. He once spent 22 minutes looking for a pocket he had put some money in.

Skimpiest Bikini

On the famous beach in St. Tropez, France, some women have been spotted wearing bikinis made of bandages and surgical gauze. The "medical look" became the rage after Miss St. Tropez showed up at the beach covered by bandages. She had stepped on a beehive.

Newest Hairdo

Brent Madison of Scranton, Pennsylvania, got back at his parents, who wouldn't let him ride a motorcycle, with a one-of-a-kind haircut. He had his head shaved except for two clumps of hair on top, which he shapes with gel so they point straight up like antennae. Kids made fun of him until two friends got the same cut. Now, there's a gang in Scranton known as "The Martians" whose members all sport Madison's hairdo.

Sermon with the Most Fire and Brimstone

Reverend L. Kamalino draws standing room only crowds during his sermons at the New Age Pacific Church in Hoolehua, Hawaii. His enormous pulpit is built of volcanic rock. At dramatic moments, Reverend Kamalino presses a button and little geysers of fake fire, brimstone, and molten lava shoot into the air.

Most Enjoyable Funeral

When Liam O'Keefe, the unpopular mayor of Tubbercurry, Ireland, passed away, the whole town went to his funeral and partied for two days. There was free food, storytelling, drinking, and dancing. Debts were forgiven and the town's prison was emptied.

Youngest Voting Age

In the Kampuchea hamlet of Paoy Pet, where children outnumber adults five to one, the minimum voting age is seven years old and the mayor is only nine. Local laws allow children to eat as much candy as they want, stay up as late as they like, and punish their parents whenever they think they've been bad.

Most Corrupt Jury Tampering

In 1933, Bert Winkler of Yazoo City, Mississippi, bribed an entire jury during his bank robbery trial. He had a friend slip each juror a note that said Winkler would give each one of them $1,000 if he was acquitted. After he was found innocent and could not be retried, he opened up a briefcase and distributed the money. Winkler was so happy, he also gave $5,000 to the judge, $250 to the bailiff, and $5 to each person who attended the trial. He handed the prosecuting attorney a nickel.

Most Pleasant Hijacking

In 1967, three bank robbers hijacked a U.S. airliner to Cuba. They gave everyone all the food they could eat and even brought pastries on board to share with the passengers. The robbers told jokes, played guitar, juggled, and chatted with everyone on board. After landing in Havana, they distributed $50,000 of their stolen money to the passengers and then disappeared, never to be found.

Largest Jailbreak

The largest jailbreak began as an innocent Christmas party. Eight prisoners in Wagga Wagga, Australia, baked a batch of Christmas cookies filled with a chocolate-flavored laxative for the warden and all the guards. While the guards were running to the bathroom, all the cells were unlocked and 362 convicts escaped.

Most Efficient Train Robbery

In 1807, a 17-car freight train was stolen by bandits near Hamtramck, Michigan. The engineer was thrown off and the train was diverted to an iron works factory, which paid the robbers $5,000 for the train, melted it down car by car, and resold it as scrap metal.

Worst Nickname for a Mobster

Salvatore Calabrese was a hitman for the violent Pellegrino mob family of Cleveland, Ohio. In exchange for a new identity and relocation through the Federal Witness Protection Program, Calabrese described 12 grisly murders he had committed, named other Mafia members in Cleveland, and admitted that his mob nickname was "Cupcake."

Least Civilized Tribe

A primitive tribe of cannibals near Sampit, Borneo, has no language and wears no clothes. They don't even peel bananas before they eat them.

HUMAN ACCOMPLISHMENTS

Longest World War II Holdout
Sadaharu Fukushima refuses to acknowledge that the Japanese surrendered at the end of World War II. He lives in a trench on the island of Guam and has surrounded himself with land mines and grenades. Although his Japanese uniform is ripped to shreds, Fukushima still wears it every day. He refuses to leave the trench until he receives orders from his commanding officer, who died 27 years ago.

Longest Imitation of Donald Duck
Twelve-year-old Jimmy McGriff of Delray Beach, Florida, has been talking like the cartoon character Donald Duck since he was two. Despite numerous treatments, doctors have determined he is no longer capable of speaking in a normal voice.

Longest Nonreligious Chant
Angus Kincaid, age nine, of Dundee, Scotland, dropped an ice cream cone and for 11 days chanted, "Give me another ice cream cone," over and over. His parents tried to quiet him. They yelled, pleaded, sent him to bed without dinner, took him to three different psychiatrists, and finally, in desperation, gave him another ice cream cone. The chanting miraculously stopped.

Worst Birthday Party
An unemployed terrorist living in Bandar Abbas, Iran, celebrated his thirtieth birthday with a group of terrorist friends. However, as the cake was carried out of the kitchen, one of the lighted candles ignited a box of C-4 plastic explo-

sives. The next day, all that could be found were bits of wood, plaster, clothing, and "Happy Birthday" wrapping paper.

Wildest Christmas Office Party

The accounting firm Bland and McMeeker of North Platte, Nebraska, held a Christmas office party that turned into an utter disaster. The event resulted in four divorces, seven fist fights, and over $30,000 in property damage. It was the first time the firm had ever held a Christmas party. It was also the last.

World's Fastest Typist

Marco Sorrento of Pisciotta, Italy, can type almost twice as fast as the next fastest typist. His secret: he types on two typewriters at the same time, using his hands on one and his feet on the other. He can also play four-handed duets on the piano, but not for long. He gets muscle cramps when he tries to keep both his feet and both his hands on a piano keyboard for more than a few minutes.

Longest Marriage Vows

Bernard Prothroe and Annamarie Kendall, two lawyers in the Hartford, Connecticut, firm of Peckinpah & Wickersham, wrote their own wedding vows. The vows covered 47 single-spaced, legal-size typewritten pages, and it took one of the firm's partners 5 hours, 12 minutes, 51 seconds to read them. By the time he finished, 90 percent of the guests, including the bride's and groom's parents, had already left.

Worst Honeymoon

Scott and Debbie Powell of Severna Park, Maryland, honeymooned on a romantic island in the South Pacific. Scott's wallet and camera were stolen, they both got dysentery, and the island's volcano erupted, forcing them to flee in outriggers to a nearby island. Sick to their stomachs, with no money and only the clothes on their backs, they spent the rest of the trip inside a cave until they were rescued.

Most Wives

Prince Zabid of Qatar has 612 wives. Since he can't remember most of their names, he makes them wear numbers on their backs. The prince is celibate. He says he marries often because he likes to eat wedding cake.

Worst Reason for a Granted Divorce

Laurel Krystyczewski of Detroit, Michigan, was granted a divorce from her husband, Leonard, in 1931. She claimed mental cruelty because he always left the toilet seat up.

Most Nervous Bridegroom

Lucio Romanelli couldn't sleep for nine days prior to his marriage to Luisa Maria Columbo in Palermo, Sicily. He suffered from nightmares, bed-wetting, and cold sweats. On the day of the wedding, Romanelli got lost on the way to the church, dropped the ring during the ceremony, and forgot to lift the veil before kissing the bride. Romanelli's wedding anxiety began the day he found out that Luisa's father was the head of a Mafia family in Sicily and strongly disapproved of the marriage.

Longest Engagement

Svetlana Korchnoi and Ivan Rostropovich of the town Novosibirsk in the Soviet Union have been engaged to be married for 41 years. Each year on their engagement anniversary, Ivan takes Svetlana out to dinner. Both are still employed at the borscht factory where they first met and say they'll wed when they can afford to move out of their parents' homes.

Fastest Cross-Country Hitchhiking Trip

Todd Morrell started hitchhiking from Quincy, Massachusetts, hoping to see some of the United States. Twenty minutes later, he was picked up as a hostage by a bank robber who was being chased by the police. After 62 hours, 16 minutes, 44 seconds of nonstop, high-speed driving, they arrived in San Diego. The bank robber was arrested at his father's house, and Morrell began hitchhiking again, hoping to see some of the United States.

Most Balloons Popped

The E.G. Bleckman Corp. of Leipzig, East Germany, threw its annual company party in a hotel ballroom decorated with 2,500 balloons. Heinrich Wiesbaden, an employee who was disgusted at receiving a turkey instead of a bonus check, spent the entire party angrily popping balloons with a ball-point pen. After destroying 1,672 balloons, Wiesbaden was finally ushered out by two security guards, and the company president took back the turkey as punishment.

Longest Film Industry Lunch

Former Century Pictures vice president of production Mel Levy and producer Barry Pearson sat down one noon for lunch at Le Bar and Grill in Los Angeles, California. After writing on 37 napkins, running up a bill of $317.50, and talking for 11 hours, they finally agreed on a deal to make a film about teenagers in love. The next week, Century's president killed the project.

Longest Last Request

Parisian murderer Gaston Gateau's last request before going to the guillotine was to be served a gourmet dinner. Gateau ordered Chicken Kiev, broccoli with bernaise sauce, potatoes au gratin, and a chocolate eclair. Gateau complained about the food and sent it back six times before he was satisfied. Then they chopped his head off.

Longest Two-Way Message in a Bottle

After being shipwrecked on Rongerik Island in the South Pacific, Amos Sloane put a note in a bottle and dropped the bottle in the ocean. His note, which told of intense heat and nothing but coconuts to eat, floated due north 5,000 miles and was picked up by a fisherman on Kodiak Island, Alaska. Nine months later, Sloane found a note in a bottle on the beach. It said: "It's 20 below here, nothing to eat but frozen fish, and I have to work for a living, so don't complain."

Longest Telephone Call

Heather Alexander and Jennifer Steffens of Yakima, Washington, spoke to each other on the phone nonstop for 22 hours while their parents were away for the weekend. The conversation concerned boys, rock music, clothes, and hair. Ironically, Heather and Jennifer live next door to each other.

Longest Time on Hold

Dan Gill called radio station WHAT-FM in Pascagoula, Mississippi, to request they play a particular rock song for his girlfriend. He was put on hold and, one hour later, he fell asleep. The next morning, nine hours later, someone at the station picked up the phone, told Dan they couldn't find the song he wanted, and hung up on him.

Rudest Telephone Operator

Myrtle Halverson is a telephone operator in Fond du Lac, Wisconsin, who always speaks in an angry voice. She never says "please" or "thank you" while working, and she shouts at people who have misplaced the number they were calling. Halverson hangs up on anyone who complains, has a question, or doesn't speak fast enough.

Most Frequent Wrong Number

When Pamela Palmer moved to Toms Rivers, New Jersey, she was assigned a phone number one digit different from the number for weather information in her area. After three months and 1,343 wrong-number phone calls, Palmer had her number changed. But her new number was similar to that of a popular pizza parlor and she received 81 calls in six days from people wanting to know if she delivered. Palmer has disconnected her phone and now uses a nearby pay phone for one hour each morning to make and receive all her calls.

Longest Sleepwalk

Pam Rhoades of Wheeling, West Virginia, set the distance record for sleepwalking. Wearing a long nightgown and curlers, Rhoades left her cabin and walked with her eyes wide open, snoring. Three days later, she was found in Lexington, Kentucky, and it took the sound of an alarm clock to wake her.

Longest Confession

Aidan O'Malley, at the age of 98, gave a nine-hour confession to a priest in a church in Cork, Ireland. His confession detailed 4,821 times he had used improper language, raised his voice in anger, or hurt others' feelings. The confession was so involved, O'Malley had to return the following week for three more hours to finish it.

Longest Search for a Parking Space

During a Fourth of July weekend, Doris Dolan drove around her neighborhood in Boston, Massachusetts, for two-and-a-half hours looking for a parking space. Needing to use the bathroom desperately, she double-parked in front of her apartment for five minutes. When she came back out, her car had been towed.

Longest Bath

During the Oktoberfest Celebration in Wildbad, West Germany, Jurgen Gerber took a six-day bath in warm beer. Gerber didn't mind smelling like beer because he works in a brewery, but his whole body became wrinkled and for three months he looked like he was at least 90 years old.

Rudest Life Insurance Agent

Garth Bliss is the top salesperson for the Ultra Security Insurance Co. of Detroit, Michigan. He uses false statistics to convince housewives that their husbands will probably die within the next six months. When potential customers refuse to buy insurance, he calls them "selfish and cheap."

Most Cosmetic Surgery

On the advice of her agent, aspiring film actress Lani Edwards of North Hollywood, California, had her tummy tucked, face lifted, nose bobbed, nostrils widened, breasts enlarged, belly button narrowed, and every blemish on her body removed by dermabrasion. But casting directors wouldn't hire her, saying she looked "too perfect." To pay off her medical bill, Edwards now works as her surgeon's secretary.

Most Inept Surgeon

On the island of Trinidad, Dr. Hector Vasconcelos once left his mask, gloves, and two surgical instruments inside a patient's stomach. When he discovered his mistake, he performed another operation to retrieve the lost instruments. Overjoyed at getting his equipment back, he forgot to sew up the patient and she died.

Stupidest Question Asked of a Wise Man

Sharlene Dwyer of Venice, California, scaled the Himalaya Mountains in Nepal for 10 days to reach the retreat of the great Indian mystic and religious leader, Pranabanda. Pranabanda at first refused to talk with her, then agreed to answer only one question. Overcome with exhaustion and hunger after her 10-day climb, Dwyer asked, "Why can't I ask more than one question?"

Clumsiest Waiter

In Waterloo, Iowa, Hattie Noff owns and runs a diner by herself. She has broken hundreds of dishes, knocked over tables, spilled soup on customers' laps, dropped ice down their shirts, and injured some by dropping silverware on them. Nevertheless, Hattie's customers love her food. Regulars show up at her diner wearing ponchos, dirty clothes, hard hats, and protective goggles.

Most Expert Wine Taster

Giuseppe Reggio of Naples, Italy, is the most knowledge-able wine taster in the world. Just by smelling a wine, Reggio can tell nine times out of ten the year, the country, the region, the vineyard, the row, and whether the grapes were picked with the left hand or the right.

Sourest Grapes

Brothers Henri and Pierre Lelouche inherited the Lelouche Wineries in Arles, France, after their father died. But when Henri won the coin toss to determine whose name was to be the first on the label, Pierre went berserk. He set fire to the vineyards, shot holes in the storage vats, and never drank wine or spoke French again.

Most Spam Eaten

Bruce Lansky of Minnetonka, Minnesota, has eaten more Spam in one sitting than anyone else. On June 1, 1988, he consumed 21 12-ounce cans in three hours, 14 minutes. Lansky got into the habit of eating large quantities of Spam while in college. He often arrived at the cafeteria late, and Spam was all that was left. As a child his parents had never allowed him to leave the table without cleaning his plate, so he hated to see all that Spam going to waste and finished it himself.

Weirdest Lunch

Peter Van Hooke of Rotterdam, Netherlands, has an insatiable appetite for earthworms. Because Van Hooke has an office job downtown, he often lunches underground at a nearby construction site.

Hungriest Cannibals

Members of a small tribe of cannibals in the jungle near the Cuchivero River in Venezuela have such big appetites that they sometimes send hunters 125 miles away to bring back someone to eat. They consume an average of six people a week and once devoured a group of eight tourists in under two-and-a-half hours. Every four years, these cannibals elect a new leader and eat the old one.

Most Health Food Eaten

At the Esalen retreat in Big Sur, California, Mandy Sontag ate seven bowls of granola, five bowls of alfalfa sprouts, six soyburgers, three bowls of plain yogurt, and two pounds of sunflower seeds at a single sitting. She drank a gallon of chamomile tea to wash it all down. To celebrate her record, Sontag ate two bags of chocolate chip cookies.

Most Careless Barber

Elvin Howlett, who runs a one-man barber shop in Murfreesboro, Tennessee, has nicked or cut 52 of his customers. The cost of his liability insurance is now so high, Howlett's trying to sell his barber business and get a job as a butcher.

Most Hotel Rooms Destroyed

A professional wrestler who goes by the name of "The Trash Compactor" destroyed 22 hotel rooms in 22 cities during a U.S. wrestling tour. He entertained his friends by throwing the room service waiters around while demonstrating different wrestling holds.

Greatest Fireworks Display

Guy Berckmans of Brussels, Belgium, was laid off from his job as a stockboy at the St. Pieter Fireworks Co. after working 18 months without a raise. He sneaked into the warehouse one night, started a fire, and treated himself and everyone within a 10-mile radius to a six-hour fireworks display featuring 450,000 colorful rockets, bombs, sparklers, and noise-makers.

Most Visits to the Dentist

Though her teeth are healthy and she flosses every day, Viktoria Leinsdorf of Graz, Austria, has gone to the dentist twice a week for the past 11 years. She loves to have her teeth cleaned and is particularly fond of the numb sensation she gets from novocaine shots.

Most Furs Owned

Countess Wilhelmina Leopold of Liechtenstein has a collection of 77 fur coats and wraps. They include mink, fox, rabbit, muskrat, ermine, and seal. Ironically, the Countess doesn't wear them often because she spends her winters on the French Riviera.

Most Shoes Owned

Antonia Podesta of Livorno, Italy, spends all her spare time and a lot of her husband's money buying shoes, new and used. She has over 2,000 pairs, filling one entire floor of their large home. She won't wear most of them outside her house, though, because she doesn't want to get them dirty.

Most Jewelry Worn at One Time

At her wedding, Princess Malité of Togo wore 12 necklaces, 10 bracelets on each arm, 25 rings on her fingers, 10 rings on her toes, 3 rings in her nose, 6 pierced earrings, a diamond tiara, and an emerald in her navel. Princess Malité, who weighed only 97 pounds before dressing for the occasion, couldn't walk down the aisle, so she was carried by two muscular bodyguards.

Most Embarrassing Clothing Rip

Princess Astrid of Luxembourg ripped her skintight gown during her coronation as the entire country watched on TV. Astrid was so embarrassed, she ran away and joined a convent. Two weeks later, her younger sister, Marta, was crowned queen.

Shortest High School Prom

The senior prom at McCallum High School in El Dorado, Arkansas, officially lasted six minutes, 36 seconds. The lead guitarist of the band knocked over a soft drink into an amplifier, which exploded, setting fire to the auditorium and causing a stampede. The theme for the prom was "Have a Hot Summer."

Cruelest Boy Scout Leader

Arthur Moncrieff led a troop of Boy Scouts in Gallup, New Mexico, until he was thrown out of the organization. Moncrieff's field trips included an obstacle course at a nearby Marine training camp and a 16-mile "nature walk" in the desert in the middle of summer while carrying 20-pound backpacks.

Fastest Opening of a Locked Car Door with a Wire Hanger

Madge Percy from Okmulgee, Oklahoma, has locked her keys in her car so many times, she is now able to stick a wire hanger through a space above the window glass and unlock the door in 3.5 seconds. She can also turn on the ignition, radio, and lights with a hanger in 23.7 seconds. Percy refuses to make herself a spare key. Instead, she carries a wire hanger with her everywhere.

Toughest Meter Monitor

In Seville, Spain, a meter monitor named Gloria Escobar writes tickets for parking violations even if the meter has just expired and the driver is in the car. Escobar dodges traffic and runs across the street if she spots a parking meter that has run out of time. She once gave out a record 387 tickets in one week and gave an additional ticket to a man who angrily protested his ticket. The offense was disorderly conduct.

Most Creative Note Used by a Bank Robber

Mustafa Hazez of Port Said, Egypt, an unemployed poet, was so in love with a teller at a local bank that he sent her love letters for three years. Receiving no answer, Hazez finally approached the teller with a gun and a long love poem, demanding that she either declare her love for him or give him all the money in her drawer. She gave him the money. Hazez was later convicted of robbery, but was given a reduced sentence of three years on a plea of temporary insanity.

Most Dangerous Security Guard

Jeb Finley of Goodnight, Texas, has worked for 19 different companies as a security guard. He has shot at cats, dogs, shadows, and swaying tree branches thinking they were burglars. Finley's worst error in judgment was sounding an alarm when he heard a strange noise and later engaging in a 15-minute shootout with the police officers who responded. Finley is no longer allowed to carry a lethal weapon, but he still works as a security guard and keeps a loaded water pistol in his holster, "just in case."

Most Disgusting Teacher's Pet

Leslie Ngambe attends junior high school in Bulawayo, Zimbabwe. His efforts to impress his teacher are so blatant that most of the other students won't talk to him anymore. Besides earning the highest grades in the class, Ngambe brings his teacher a flower each day. Even more annoying to the other students, Ngambe carries his teacher's books, cleans the chalkboard, opens doors for her, and has been spotted outside her house washing her car.

Child with the Most Toys

Clancy Murdock, the only son of British publishing magnate Maxwell Murdock, has a two-story playhouse filled with toys. Among the $2.5 million in playthings are a platinum go-kart, an F-14 fighter jet-flight simulator, and a 12-foot-tall, remote-control dinosaur named Rex. Clancy has instructed his butler to walk Rex around the block twice each day.

Most Intimidating School Principal

Al Carbone is the six-foot, two-inch, 240-pound principal of John Wayne High School in Orange County, California. If he catches someone smoking, he makes the student put the cigarette out and eat it. Carbone often has to break up fights between students, so he carries an electric cattle prod with him at all times.

Most Entertaining School Crossing Guard

Celia Calduron is a crossing guard at an elementary school in San Juan, Puerto Rico. She wears a custom-made, red, white, and blue uniform and tap shoes, so she can tap dance while she leads kids across the street. Calduron also plays harmonica, sings songs, and twirls the stop sign she holds.

Worst School Bully

Bart Conran is the terror of Canberra, Australia. Although he is only 15, Bart is six feet, five inches tall, weighs 246 pounds, and beats up any student who annoys him. The principal lectured him once, but Bart beat him senseless and tore up his office, so nothing more has been said.

Most Macho Name

Butch Duke Biff Rex Harding is the only child of Mr. and Mrs. Lonnie Harding of Fergus Falls, Minnesota. Surprisingly, Butch Duke Biff Rex is a girl. She was given the name because the Hardings wanted a boy.

Most Talkative Bridge Tolltaker

Paulette Perot works as a bridge tolltaker in Marseilles, France. She is extremely outgoing, chatting with each driver who pays the toll. When asked for directions, Perot often draws detailed maps and suggests scenic routes, restaurants, and local wineries to visit. Perot has been known to talk to drivers for up to 10 minutes, creating traffic jams that back up three or four miles.

Greediest Head of State

The seventh-century Roman ruler Augustus III allowed any man who paid him at least 50 gold pieces to become a senator. By the end of his reign, the Roman Senate had grown to 642 members, so meetings were moved from the senate building to the Coliseum.

Least Successful Hit Man

The legendary Mafia hit man Benny "The Bungler" Puchetti didn't kill a single person in his brief career. His many failures included forgetting to load his gun, slipping and hitting his head on the bathtub while trying to choke someone in a shower, tripping and falling on his own knife, and finally, driving off a cliff while trying to run a victim off the road.

Worst Killjoy

Hilda Ruiz is a professional chaperone for high school students in Camagüey, Cuba, and a general killjoy. She has interrupted 117 kisses, 32 cases of heavy petting, and 19 cases of other things. Ruiz does not permit young couples to hold hands or even touch until they are married.

Most Gullible Person

Jean-Phillipe Beauregard of Port-au-Prince, Haiti, not only believes in voodoo, but in Santa Claus and the Tooth Fairy as well. There is usually a line in front of his house as door-to-door peddlers, fund-raisers, and charlatans wait their turn to separate him from his hard-earned money.

Most Citations for Indecent Exposure

Helga Svenstrup of Copenhagen, Denmark, has been arrested 45 times for indecent exposure. The spunky 67-year-old even received a jail sentence for flashing a judge. During halftime at a sold-out soccer match, she ran onto the field dressed as a cheerleader and performed cartwheels without any underwear. The crowd of 50,000 cheered.

Worst Litterbug

Donna Galdi of Passaic, New Jersey, never uses garbage cans. She dumps her garbage directly onto the street from her second floor apartment and has been fined 83 times for public littering. She considers littering "public art," like graffiti, and once filled a phone booth with her old coffee grounds.

Best-Smelling Author

Although he is not yet a best-selling author, Brad Schreiber, a writer in Los Angeles, California, does have the distinction of being the best-smelling author. Schreiber collected 137 bottles of cologne, perfume, toilet water, aftershave lotion, and scented bath oil from his friends; dumped the contents into his tub; and bathed in it for 13 hours, 24 minutes, 18 seconds. Schreiber has not used any underarm deodorant since his aromatic bath.

Biggest Movie Fan

Barney Roth of Greeley, Colorado, has seen all the *Rambo* films a total of 494 times in movie theaters. When he goes to see one of the films, he wears battle fatigues, grease-paint, and a headband and carries a registered though unloaded assault rifle. Roth mimics all of Rambo's lines, shouts, and grunts, to the immense displeasure of those sitting near him.

Fastest Car Jack

Don Mabley is a service station mechanic in Shreveport, Louisiana, who doesn't need to use a jack when he changes a tire. He just picks up the car with one hand and changes the tire with the other. Mabley, a former professional wrestler, quit the ring when he was body slammed by Bo "Bulldozer" Rozier.

Most Persistent Evangelist

In the St. Louis, Missouri, airport Anita Trevithick, an evangelist, hands people flowers and booklets about her religion. If people accept the items, Trevithick follows them around the airport, waits with them at their gate, bus stop, or even outside the restroom until they contribute money or sign a membership card. Trevithick has occasionally followed people onto planes and delayed departures, refusing to leave until she receives a contribution.

Cleverest Guru

Sri Pandi runs a religious commune in Eugene, Oregon. When followers arrive, they give him all their worldly possessions, and he says, "Now that you have nothing, you have nothing to worry about."

Greatest Crashing Bore

Lord Graydon Pembroke, sixth Earl of Halifax, could clear an entire ballroom by talking endlessly about his ingrown toenails. The term "crashing bore" is attributed to him because, when he began one of his long speeches, servants dropped their trays of china or wine glasses, hoping the noise would make him stop. It never did.

Most Overprotective Mother

Merle Merton's mother, Alana, of Millinocket, Maine, cooks for her son, cleans his clothes, tucks him in at night, and will not let him date anyone, even though Merle is 55 years old. While Merle is at work, Alana calls once every two hours to make sure he's feeling well and to see if he has eaten the brown bag lunch she made for him.

Most Annoying Mother-in-Law

For 13 years, Margaret O'Brien of Londonderry, Northern Ireland, constantly told her daughter she had married a "no-good slob." O'Brien spied on her son-in-law and spread rumors about him. Finally, her daughter divorced the son-in-law and announced she was going to marry a Protestant man. O'Brien, a strict Catholic, had a heart attack and is still in critical condition.

Most Loving Son

Dr. Raymond Tolbert, an archaeology professor at the University of Virginia, was very attached to his mother. When she died, he was deeply depressed until he embalmed her and wrapped her up like a mummy. Now he takes her with him wherever he goes, and his depression has been cured.

Bus Driver with the Worst Sense of Direction

Jesus Maté of Luzon City, Philippines, has been driving the same bus route for six years, and he still gets lost several times a week. Passengers have to remind him where to turn. Fist fights often break out when passengers argue over which way to go.

Noisiest Trash Collector

Hoagy Bostwick, a Philadelphia, Pennsylvania, trash collector, has a booming voice, a painfully loud belch, and often disturbs people who live along his route by banging drumsticks on metal garbage cans.

ATHLETICS AND HOBBIES

Worst Car Race Pit Crew

The pit crew for Mexican racer Pepe "Speedy" Gonzalez is not very proficient. They once poured gas into the radiator and water into the gas tank. One crew member got stuck under the car for 10 minutes. Their most spectacular blunder was forgetting to tighten the lugnuts after changing Gonzalez's tires. When he sped away from the pit, all four tires went flying off in different directions.

Most Outrageous-Looking Dragster

"Loony" Louie Belcher of Twentynine Palms, California, drives a 625-horsepower dragster that looks like a giant banana slug on wheels. "The Lazy Slug" is bright yellow and has two antennae on the hood that wiggle. Belcher's cockpit is in the shell. Although the dragster is sponsored by a major pesticide company, most racetracks think the Lazy Slug is ugly and won't allow it at their events. So, Belcher makes most of his money appearing at flower shows.

Deepest Ground Ball

After a week of heavy rain, the infield was soggy when Pete Lawrence of the Collegeville (Tennessee) Woodchucks hit a ball eight inches into the ground. The catcher couldn't dig the ball out of the muddy infield as Lawrence rounded the bases. The umpires called it a ground rule double.

Strangest Home Run

Jarvis Strock of the Rochester (Minnesota) Robins, a minor league baseball team, hit a line drive that stuck to the cleats on the left shoe of the pitcher. While the pitcher tried to pry the ball loose, Strock circled the bases and headed for home.

The catcher pulled the shoe off the pitcher's foot and raced back to home plate, tagging Strock out. But the umpire ruled that the catcher had tagged him with the shoe, not the ball, so Strock was awarded an inside-the-park home run.

Longest Argument During a Softball Game

During a "friendly" softball game in Pocatello, Idaho, a runner tried to break a 1-1 tie in the bottom of the ninth inning by sliding under a catcher's tag. The runner's team claimed he was safe; the opponents insisted he was out. Both teams screamed at each other for two hours, 21 minutes, until it was so dark they could no longer see whom they were yelling at. After the game, they went to a local restaurant and argued for two more hours until the restaurant closed.

Slowest Base Runner

Kenji Saku weighed 320 pounds when he played first base for the Osaka Otters of Japan. Saku was so slow, he had to hit a double or triple to get safely to first base. When he hit a home run, it took him two minutes, 30 seconds to waddle around the bases because he needed to stop and rest at each one.

Highest Pop Fly

Waylon Harkness of Lubbock, Texas, hit a towering pop fly that landed in the back seat of a crop duster flying 525 feet overhead. When the players couldn't find the ball, a priest walked onto the field and led the crowd in a minute of silent prayer, and then the game continued.

Shortest Boxing Title Fight

Roberto Banducci lost his Italian heavyweight championship belt to Pietro Lambordozzi in Naples, Italy, before the opening bell sounded. Banducci was waiting in the ring when

Lambordozzi entered the arena with Banducci's ex-girlfriend on his arm. Banducci, wild with rage, jumped out of the ring, hit Lambordozzi over the head with a chair, and threw him into the scorer's table, knocking him unconscious. The judges immediately voted to strip Banducci of his title, and Lambordozzi became champion after being knocked out.

Most Knockouts in One Fight

Andor Zimmermann and Sasha Gabor had a wild brawl in Szeged, Hungary. Although neither boxer was hurt, they did manage to knock out three referees. Two judges, the time-keeper, and the ring announcer tried keeping the fight under control, but at the end of seven rounds and seven officials, it was declared a draw.

Most Skateboarding Injuries

Rhonda Redmond of Kalispell, Montana, continues to skateboard after 31 serious accidents. She has been run over by cars, trucks, motorcycles, joggers, and once by a mother pushing twins in a baby carriage.

Most Temperamental Flamenco Dancer

Enrique Nava of Alicante, Spain, has such a bad temper, he kicks over the tables of people not watching him when he performs. Offstage he is just as bad, shouting and stamping his feet, flamenco style, when he disagrees with someone or can't get his way. While performing, Nava has broken the toes of four female dancers, claiming they deserved it because they were trying to steal the show.

Longest Locker-Room Pep Talk

Brady Bradshaw, head coach of the Newton Grove, North Carolina, high school football team, gave his players a six-hour pep talk prior to a big game with their longtime rival.

Coach Bradshaw assembled the team at 8:00 A.M. and told them how he worked during the Depression, supported his 13 brothers and sisters, never had a winning season as a player or coach, and was nagged by chronic lower-back pain. The Newton Grove team was so depressed by kickoff time that they were trounced 81-3.

Worst Weather During a Football Game

Two highly competitive junior high school coaches in Neptune Beach, Florida, insisted their teams finish a game during a hurricane. Playing in eight inches of water and gale-force winds, neither team scored in regulation time, although one goal-post was hit by lightning, four players were knocked out by flying debris, and one player needed artificial respiration after inhaling too much water. During the sudden-death play-off, a powerful gust of wind carried a small running back 12 yards into the end zone for a touchdown, ending the game.

Phoniest Wrestling Match

A bout between Mutilator Murphy and the Human Hacksaw in Sumter, South Carolina, was stopped when the Human Hacksaw held up what appeared to be Mutilator Murphy's left eyeball. After the fight, doctors found that no damage had been done to Murphy's eye. The Human Hacksaw later admitted he had smuggled a cocktail onion into the ring.

Ugliest Hockey Player

Boris Vladovich, goalie for the Soviet Union's Siberia Walruses, is missing 12 teeth and has a glass eye and a metal plate in his head. He has 39 stitches on his face, and his left ear is four inches higher than his right. Vladovich's nose has been broken so many times in play that it lies flat against the rest of his face, distorting his voice to such an extent that only proficient lip-readers can understand what he is saying.

Most Hazardous Lie

Trent Roberts of Eden Prairie, Minnesota, playing in his first PGA tournament, had bad luck on the eighth hole of the

Hazelnut Country Club course. Swinging a nine iron from the rough, his shot hit a spectator behind the head and nestled down between the back of his neck and his shirt. Roberts, unsure of the rules, asked the spectator to bend down and then chipped the ball just two feet away from the cup for an easy putt. Unfortunately, the spectator suffered a mild concussion for his troubles, and Roberts was banned from the tour for a year.

Most Challenging Golf Course

The atoll of Hao in the Pacific Ocean has the toughest 18-hole golf course. Caddies carry machetes, and golfers must avoid hazards such as lava flows, quicksand traps, and jungle birds that swoop down and pick up golf balls they think are their eggs. The tee for one hole is on one island and the cup on another. A glass-bottomed boat helps golfers locate their lost balls. Par for the course is 312.

Most Dangerous Golfer

Manny Neufeld, playing 18 holes of golf in Riverside, California, hit 14 spectators, two caddies, a chipmunk, and a blue jay. His most spectacular shot sailed over a fence and shattered the windshield of a car on a nearby highway, causing a six-car pileup. Neufeld received so much media attention that an insurance company paid him $10,000 to appear in a TV commercial.

Most Violent Fans

The soccer stadium in Maracaibo, Venezuela, has been burned to the ground three times by angry fans disappointed by the performance of their soccer teams. A metal detector was recently installed at the gate to catch fans carrying bombs, guns, and knives. As a result of increased police security, fans usually wait until the end of the match before beating up players or referees.

Weirdest Motorcycle Stunts

Rollie Briscoe of Metairie, Louisiana, wearing a cowboy hat on top of his motorcycle helmet, stood on the seat of his moving motorcycle and roped and tied a calf running in an open field. In Pocomoke City, Maryland, Billy Jo Durphee drove her Harley Davidson up a ramp, flew 50 feet in the air, and landed in a swimming pool filled with strawberry Jell-O.

Most Backboards Shattered

Arthur Troy, a six-foot, eight-inch, 275-pound high school junior from Bridgeport, Connecticut, has smashed 16 backboards with his powerful dunk shots. He now wears gloves to protect his hands, and his father has taken out a special insurance policy that protects Troy against flying glass.

Fastest 800-Meter Burning-Baton Relay

A team of four sprinters ran the 800-meter burning-baton relay in Joplin, Missouri, in 39.7 seconds. Runners in this event are not allowed to wear gloves. They have to toss the flaming baton quickly from hand to hand to reduce scorching.

Most Dangerous Track-and-Field Event

The national track-and-field championships on the island of New Caledonia include a hazardous event called the Lava Pit Long Jump. Many promising long jumpers have ended their careers early by getting off a bad jump and landing one or both feet in the red-hot volcanic lava. Now most jumpers who compete in the event wear knee-high boots made of asbestos.

Wildest Daredevil

Maynard Neeley of Butter Creek, Wyoming, has attempted feats no sane person would consider, including riding bareback on a great white shark, walking blindfolded on a tightrope over an active volcano, brushing the teeth of an angry crocodile, running back and forth across a busy interstate highway at night, and replacing a TV tube with wet hands while the set was still turned on. Neeley no longer performs stunts because he broke his back when he slipped on a bar of soap in the shower.

Biggest Gamble

Out of money, but positive he had a winning poker hand, Noah Davis of Ballarat, Australia, bet his home, two cars, fishing boat, golden retriever, and season tickets to his hometown soccer team. After Davis lost, the lucky winner felt sorry for him and let him keep the soccer tickets.

Longest Bucking Bronco Ride

Darrell Dale of Elk City, Oklahoma, had a cruel joke played on him by his fellow ranchhands. They put some superglue on the saddle of a wild bronco named Nightmare that Darrell was about to ride. After 20 minutes of being violently whipped around, Darrell pulled off his boots, unbuckled his belt, and went flying out of his pants and off of Nightmare.

Worst Names for Horses

The states of Kentucky and Virginia get credited not only for the most racehorses, but for the most tasteless racehorse names: Horsemeat Jr., Happy Hooves, Bag O' Bones, Nag Nag Nag, Born Loser, Three Legs and a Prayer, and Horse-Apples.

Closest Dead Heat

In the Anthrax Derby held in Paducah, Kentucky, a photo finish showed Hot to Trot and Hyperactive reaching the wire at the same moment. A week later, a photography lab magnified the picture 25 times, but still no winner could be determined. Finally, NASA's Jet Propulsion Lab computer analyzed the photo and proved Hyperactive had won by 1/1,000,000 of an inch. The prize money was only $10,000, and the computer analysis cost the racetrack $58,000.

Heaviest Jockey

Dawson Rutherford of Pleasure Ridge Park, Kentucky, owned his own racehorse, Sad Sadie, and rode her despite his weight of 312 pounds. Sad Sadie came in dead last in 10 straight races, sometimes stopping and refusing to move until Rutherford got off. After 10 losses, Rutherford retired as a jockey and let his son Marvin, who weighs only 255 pounds, ride Sad Sadie.

Fastest Jockey

Victor Spinoza of Hialeah, Florida, is not only a fast jockey on horseback, he is also fast on foot. Spinoza outran a field of nine thoroughbreds and riders in a 100-meter dash in 9.173 seconds, beating his own horse, Whipping Post, by a foot in a photo finish.

Most Dangerous Rodeo Event

The annual rodeo in Tulsa, Oklahoma, boasts an event called Bull Kissing. To compete, cowboys walk up to an angry Brahma bull, wrap their arms around the bull's neck, and kiss it on the mouth. The cowboy with the fewest broken bones wins.

Largest Collection of Trained Insects

Felicity Whitman of Tubac, Arizona, loves to teach insects tricks. She has trained a swarm of bees to land on her head in the shape of a hat. Whitman has also taught the ants in her ant farm to eat geometric shapes out of a piece of lettuce. Her most impressive accomplishment is getting a group of spiders to build a web that has the word "Hi" spun into it.

Most Difficult Crossword Puzzles

The School of Journalism at Oxford University in England prints a crossword puzzle each quarter. Clues include foreign words, anagrams, obscure slang, and technical jargon. In the last 21 years, only four people have completed any of their crossword puzzles.

Most Complex Bridge Codes

Alton and Jennie Sedgwick of Nottingham, England, have worked out 205 secret signals to use when they play bridge. Among them are picking their noses, belching, cracking a knuckle, and knocking over a drink on the table.

Largest Toenail Clipping Collection

Buster Lamont of Tupelo, Mississippi, has a collection of 625 mason jars filled with his toenail clippings. He has been sitting on his porch cutting his toenails and putting the clippings into jars for 37 years. The collection lines one wall of his living room.

Most Successful Sewer Fisherman

Larry Harper of Oshkosh, Wisconsin, has been fishing in the sewers of Oshkosh for seven years. In that time, he has caught 74 fish, 13 rats, 5 old shoes, and a tennis racket. Harper once also caught a small alligator, which ate a tuna fish sandwich Harper had brought for lunch and then went back down into the sewer.

Oddest Bait Used to Catch Fish

Nettie Connally of Mercer Island, Washington, has had great success for more than a decade with her customized fish bait. She starts with cheddar cheese-flavored popcorn and coats it liberally with Beluga caviar and some spices. It sells very well, too, because buyers often wind up eating most of the bait themselves and have to buy more for the fish.

How to Survive High School...with Minimal Brain Damage

by Doug Lansky & Aaron Dorfman

This is the hilarious guide for high school students that Ferris Bueller would have written, if he wasn't so busy making a movie. It contains hundreds of pranks, hoaxes and dirty tricks. It's "the greatest invention for high school kids since Cliffs Notes."
— Dave Barry.

Order #4050

Professor Percival Pinkerton's Most Perplexing Puzzles

by Christopher Maslanka

This cleverly written and illustrated book of brainteasers boasts a wide variety of math, science, logic and verbal puzzles. It also includes helpful hints and solutions.

Order #6070

Free Stuff for Kids, 1990 Edition

by the Free Stuff Editors

The completely revised and updated 13th edition features more than 350 terrific free and up-to-a-dollar items that kids can send away for by mail. It's one of the all-time best-selling children's activity books with over 1.3 million copies sold.

Order #2190

Webster's Dictionary Game
by Wilbur Webster

Dictionary Game fans will love this wacky word game invented by the black sheep of the famous dictionary family. It includes a special dictionary of over 5,000 esoteric words.
Order #6030

The Eat a Pet Cookbook
by Russel Jones

Finally a cookbook for those who really mean it when they say, "I could eat a horse." So outrageous, *101 Things to Do with a Dead Cat* seems tame by comparison. Jones' mouth-watering recipes include Goldfish Gumbo, Kitten Crunch, Bunny Burgers, Chihuahua Chili and Rib of Rover.
Order #4180

Strange But True Facts About Sex
by David Smith and Mike Gordon

Here's a book about sex that even Doctor Ruth could learn from. It contains strange but true and often hilarious facts from history, anthropology, medicine, and Hollywood gossip. Outrageous fun for trivia buffs and anyone fascinated by sex.
Order #4240

Order Form

Qty	Title	Author	Order No.	Unit Cost	Total
	Almost Grown-Up	Patterson, C.	2290	$4.95	
	Eat a Pet Cookbook	Jones, R.	4180	$6.95	
	Empty Nest Symphony	McBride, M.	4080	$4.95	
	Dads Say the Dumbest Things	Lansky, Jones	4220	$5.95	
	How to Be a Catholic Mother	Dodds, B.	4230	$4.95	
	How to Survive High School	Lansky/Dorfman	4050	$5.95	
	Italian Without Words	Cangelosi/Carpini	5100	$4.95	
	L.I.A.R.	Thornton, R.	4070	$4.95	
	Modern Girl's Guide to Everything	Cooke, K.	4090	$4.95	
	Mother Murphy's Law	Lansky, B.	1149	$3.50	
	Mother Murphy's 2nd Law	Lansky, B.	4010	$3.50	
	Parents' Guide to Dirty Tricks	Dodds, B.	4190	$4.95	
	Playing Fast & Loose with Time & Space	Mueller, P.	4100	$4.95	
	Prof. Pinkerton's Most Perplexing Puzzles	Maslanka, C.	6070	$4.95	
	Prof. Pinkerton's Best Brain Busters	Maslanka, C.	6110	$4.95	
	Strange But True Facts About Sex	Smith/Gordon	4240	$6.95	
	Wall Street Bull	Lansky, B.	4040	$4.95	
	Weird Wonders, Bizarre Blunders	Schreiber, B.	4120	$4.95	
	Webster's Dictionary Game	Webster, W.	6030	$5.95	
	Wordplay	Thiesen/King	2200	$5.95	

Subtotal	
Shipping and Handling (see below)	
MN residents add 6% sales tax	
Total	

Meadowbrook Press

YES, please send me the books indicated above. Add $1.25 shipping and handling for the first book and $.50 for each additional book. Add $2.00 to total for books shipped to Canada. Overseas postage will be billed. Allow up to 4 weeks for delivery. Send check or money order payable to Meadowbrook Press. No cash or C.O.D.'s please. Quantity discounts available upon request. Prices are subject to change without notice.

Send book(s) to:

Name_____

Address_____

City_____ State_____ Zip_____

☐ Check enclosed for $_____, payable to Meadowbrook Press
☐ Charge to my credit card (for purchases of $10.00 or more only)
☐ Phone Orders call: (800) 338-2232 (for purchases of $10.00 or more only)

Account #_____ ☐ Visa ☐ MasterCard

Signature_____ Exp. date_____